Public Education:
The Modern-Day Lynching Tree

Rometha Gilmore, M. Ed.
Mrs. Educator

Public Education: The Modern-Day Lynching Tree

Copyright © 2023 by Rometha Gilmore

All rights reserved. No part of this book may be reproduced or transmitted in any form or by any means without written permission from the author.

ISBN (979-8-9862446-9-3)

MTE Publishing
mtepublishing.com

Table of Contents

Acknowledgements & Dedication iv

Introduction: Integration Did Not Remove the Noose vi

Chapters

1. My MOST Impressionable Years: My Experiences as a Student in Public Education. 1

2. Greater Than, Less Than, & Equal *Too*… 4

3. Life Tests within Public Education 14

4. Educational Freedom: College Bound 25

5. The Struggle within My Calling 31

6. Reading, wRiting, aRithmetic & Racism 43

7. Appointed the New House ~~Nigger~~ Administrator 47

8. Pain in Promotion 56

9. All Educated Out: BLACKed Out, Burnt Out, Pushed Out 63

About the Author 76

Acknowledgements & Dedication

This book is dedicated to my sons, Eddie, Jamie, and Jyron. My story would not have been possible had it not been for them. As a teenage mother, they pushed me to do better, to want better and now I AM because of them. As successful young Black men, their lives are a testament to what God can and will do when we believe!

To my covering, my lover, my man, my high school sweetheart, my destined life-partner, Mr. Jamie D. Gilmore Sr., I appreciate and love you beyond words. The late nights, early mornings, trips to Gainesville have paid off.

Thank you to my maternal and paternal grandmothers Lorene and Louise (now in their eighties), who were willing to share their childhood stories and schooling.

Thank you to my mother, Mazella Tomlin, for her love and support along the way. I managed to keep my book a secret, but I know she is super proud of me.

Thank you to everyone who allowed me to interview them. Every nugget you all shared helped me make sense of the thoughts and articulate into my first book.

I must also thank all the educators who can relate, those who have been silenced, felt marginalized, singled out and oppressed; yet you've persevered for the sake of our students, our future.

Last, but not least, I'm grateful for the people and places that refused to give me space and pushed me out! God's word declares, He will make my enemies my footstool. Therefore, I will bless them, and pray for them.

Introduction:
Integration Did Not Remove the Noose

Jeremiah 1:5 (NLT) "I knew you before I formed you in your mother's womb. Before you were born, I set you apart and appointed you as my prophet to the nations."

I attended Madison Street Elementary School in Ocala, FL. I walked approximately fifteen minutes to school from Marion Manor, a cream-colored subsidized housing community (the projects). It was one of three project complexes (NH Jones, Parkside) located on 4th street; one could say the "main strip."

My school was predominantly Black, but that would soon come to an end. I entered the education plantation in 1981, and my school was upgraded to a magnet school about three to four years later. This brought on a change, a facelift one might say. Followed by another and another, making the school predominately white in the coming years.

Our classrooms were officially integrated in Marion county in 1968, under the "Freedom of Choice" plan. Ironically, it seemed as though the noose didn't loosen but it became tighter. Once integration happened, it seemed mandatory for us (Blacks) to walk on our tiptoes to avoid choking.

We had to learn *their* history and had to forsake our own as we were forced to assimilate in every capacity. Today, Public Education is indoctrinated with the asinine ideology of Critical Race Theory (CRT). Marcus Garvey once said, A people without the knowledge of their past history, origin and culture is like a tree planted without roots. Everything about being Black within education screams, "You belong in the "white room," which is nothing more than a modern-day plantation."

My mama raised my two siblings and I in a three-bedroom apartment in Marion Manor. I was the oldest. I was always eager to learn, and I loved attending school. Mama warned us daily to follow the rules. She insisted that we keep our mouths closed and pay close attention to all of our teachers.

It was no secret, she knew we were all so opinionated, getting our education would behoove us. Being outspoken, especially as a Black female, was and still is shunned. We are considered *troublemakers* by far if we choose to believe the reports of the majority. America was not built for us to have a voice. Even in my youth, I struggled with being silent, because I knew my opinion mattered. I mattered!

However, mama understood the importance of us getting a "good education", because our reality wouldn't let us get a pass. That wasn't a problem for me (at least not in the beginning), but my brother, the middle-child, suffered from middle child syndrome, and he lived up to it. I can remember mama staying on him like white on rice. She understood the plight of being Black and male. Therefore, it was imperative for my brother to get his education, so that he could rise above the negative stigmas Black men encounter daily.

Mama had already witnessed things that were unimaginable to me, even more unthinkable to my seed that would be later birthed into this unforgiving world. My younger sister managed to make it through school without many problems. Even if she didn't, the baby somehow always got a pass. She could create and cause some of the most heinous acts and still survived having to get her own switch off the tree.

I am thankful for the Black teachers I had. They did more than educate us; they loosened the noose by giving us more than "book smarts." They instilled resiliency, a strong sense of hope, confidence, and the ability to think critically—they knew our reality, the mountains we'd climb were taller and much steeper than we could ever imagine.

Our teachers were gracefully compassionate and beyond understanding, simply put…they loved us, and we knew it. They looked like us and some lived in the surrounding neighborhoods,

Jones Side, Tucker Hill, Coward Park, Richmond Heights, Happiness Homes.

Looking back, I realize they also had nooses dangling on their necks; and they saw the child-sized nooses on ours. Thus, they refused to be the culprits of our demise— educationally, emotionally, physically, and historically. Just like our ancestors, they too knew how to make the plantation life *look* livable to our young eyes, while understanding every move we made loosened or tightened the dangling nooses around our necks.

Chapter 1

My MOST Impressionable Years: My Experiences as a Student in Public Education.

Education is the key to unlock the golden door of freedom
~George Washington Carver

My 13-year journey as a student in Public Education was one of assimilation, white-washed dissemination, and an attempted obliteration of my identity. Ironically, this is the same blueprint of suppression that was ideal on plantations. Maliciously, systematic racism is the brand that sells dreams and violently assaults us with reality!

Lynching occurred daily on plantations. These horrendous acts caused our ancestors' bodies to capitulate to their circumstances. It's hard not to imagine they transitioned to a better place to escape the living hell they endured on earth.

Interestingly enough, 13 symbolizes death, but purposely it leads to rebirth because one's spirit can never be destroyed. We don't just have angels watching over us, our ancestors are literally ensuring that our purpose is fulfilled. They are the cloud of witnesses who went before us, while they continually pave the way for us... let's call it divine destiny.

Ms. Daisy Rembert, a Black woman, was my second-grade teacher who epitomized the essence of our ancestors. She believed in me and all of her students. I saw myself in her, and she treated me like I was her own. She commanded the classroom. Respect was given to her because she earned it. It's amazing how life comes full circle, because the same Daisy who taught me came back and substituted in my classroom on several different occasions. Most teachers don't leave assessments for substitutes, but that was not the case for me with Mrs. Rembert. She still commanded the classroom some twenty years later. I was confident in her and knew my students were in good hands.

After I was promoted to third grade, my school was integrated. Madison Street became Madison Street Academy. All of a sudden, my world went white. Droves of white students and white teachers took over my Black neighborhood school, and things became different, immediately. Even the school's leadership was different...

This was my official induction into the white room. Suddenly, everything was wrong with the way we learned and behaved, and everything was right because they were white. They changed what we ate, read, and learned. Our reality was instantly changed. Changes were made quickly to take us back to the plantation mentality. They decisively suppressed our common sense and incited their nonsense.

Take the Noose Off Challenge: Reflect on diversity (including/involving all students), equality (providing same resources and opportunities), equity (fairness), and inclusion (DEI) in your teachings. Education is more beneficial when inclusion and diversity are taught from non-biased lenses. Educators cannot be liabilities; we must provide stability in order to be an asset, especially to those who are already excluded while trying to exist in the white rooms.

Chapter 2

Greater Than, Less Than, & Equal *Too...*

If you are neutral in situations of injustice,
you have chosen the side of the oppressors
~Desmond Tutu

I realized early in my childhood that education was a way of life, and it was never just exclusively inside the classroom! So, I had to be GREATER, even if THEY never cultivated it. My mama always said, *"Romet, you will ALWAYS have to work TWICE as hard to get half as far as them to get the same job, and most times without the same benefits!"*

The math concept of learning greater than, less than, and equal to, never seemed so real. Therefore, by the time I was 10-years-old, I observed lessons in inequality daily from my white teachers and peers. Some of our babies, unknowingly, experience these behaviors in their preschool years. My white peers were treated as the students who were greater than and I immediately knew I was considered less than (and would never be equal to them). At least, that's how I was made to feel. We often learn through observation and understand through experience. This is an unfortunate truth for many minority students.

My fourth-grade year, we moved out of the projects to Pavilion Oaks Apartments, another low income housing complex, an upgrade from the projects. Zoned for Oakcrest Elementary, we would make that long trek to school. Sometimes a shorter walk when mama had time to drop us off to my aunt's house in Deer Run. My teacher was Mr. Touchton. Mr. Touchton was an older white man with a beard, glasses, and a Santa Claus belly. This was the same year in which the Challenger exploded, making it an unforgettable year.

Initially, we watched the shuttle launch on the TV, situated on the computer cart. Then, our class transitioned outside in the freezing cold to get a more personalized view. Shortly after liftoff, the explosion happened. Boom! Time froze! All across America everyone (including me) thought ... There are people on that shuttle, including a teacher and Ronald McNair, a Black man.

Ronald McNair was the second African American to visit space. He visited space for the first time in 1984 and again on that fatal mission in 1985. His seemingly untimely death was heartbreaking and the failure to properly memorialize him was even worse. There are numerous influential Black innovators and intellectuals that could be recognized in classrooms; yet educational oppression continues to spotlight the same individuals: Dr. Martin Luther King, Madam CJ Walker, Nelson Mandela, Mary McCleod Bethune, Mae Jemison, and Harriet Tubman. We MUST remove the nooses, NOW!

There are so many more accomplished African Americans that need to be added to the list like Phillis Wheatley, Alex Haley, Charles Drew, Guion Bluford and Fannie Lou Hammer just to name a few. Education is one of the most isolating systems, yet it is deemed all-inclusive. This is a whole lie. The system of American public education cannot teach what it does not embrace— equality.

Ironically, in 1959, when Ronald McNair was nine-years-old, he was denied the right to check out books at a segregated library, in South Carolina. Not only was he refused books, but the police were called because he was accused of causing a "disturbance."

Despite this absurdity, Ronald remained at the library and waited for the police to arrive. The officers let him go and he left with his books. There's nothing disturbing about wanting to learn; however, it's irrefutably disturbing to be denied the right to learn.

Ronald's desire for reading was the catalyst that fueled his passion for physics, engineering, and aeronautical space science.

He went on to graduate from North Carolina A&T University and earned a Ph.D. in physics from MIT (one of the most prestigious technological universities in the world). In 2011, that same public library that attempted to deny him the right to read was renamed the Dr. Ronald E. McNair Life History Center.

Interestingly enough, while reading his story, I recalled an unexpected encounter with a librarian at a school where I once worked in 2017. Although I cannot recall what initiated our conversation, I will never forget the librarian's honest yet seemingly incomprehensible statement, "I don't know how to teach Black kids…"

I was flabbergasted, and almost speechless. However, I asked, "What do you mean by that?" Of course, much more than that was said in my head. Not only was she a certified teacher, but she was employed at a Title I school and teaching intensive reading classes! Unsurprisingly, a vast majority of minority students are placed in intensive classes. I have no clue what her response was because I had completely zoned out.

I could only imagine how many Black students she refused to educate because of her ignorance. We know and understand the power that lies between those pages. In 2021, this same librarian smacked a student's hand because he refused to stand and say the pledge of allegiance. Coincidence? No, this is the reality of public education. This speaks volumes for who she is and what she stands for. The plantation mentality has been welcomed into our schools and classrooms for years. It's often disguised or overlooked while white patriarchal supremacy and privilege continues to wreak havoc in our education system.

That was a defining moment for me. As an educator it has always been my mission to continue working to ensure Black students are given a fair chance to become equal to their white peers. However, it wouldn't come without a battle from those who looked like me *and* those who didn't. I learned early on in my teaching career that the white room is considered the right way and only way to attain any kind of peace and perceived success.

I can certainly say I have experienced my share of classroom burnout due to a myriad of things that were out of my control such as state mandates, district requirements, school expectations, county/campus politics and a lack of parental support. I needed a new experience. What could I do to make an impact beyond the classroom? I applied to multiple jobs outside of teaching, but I was often turned down and received mass/canned email responses.

Eventually, after 12 years of serving in the classroom, I was promoted to serving in a quasi-administration position as a dean. Society is always screaming about having experience, but how can I gain experience if never given a chance to experience it (the thing or the job). Then a little short white guy in stature but strong in voice and presence, Mr. Jennings gave me a chance. I attempted to make things equal by addressing disciplinary issues, blind to the fact that it was an uphill battle. I thought it would be a relatively easy fix, but to my dismay, the opposite was my new reality. So, I worked diligently with my team to improve the existing system that would work across the board for all students, regardless of race.

I was excited about the opportunity to climb the public education ladder (so I thought). I believed in education, I was the student, teacher and now in leadership as a dean, where I thought I could create positive change. However, I was quickly reminded that I was still in the white room, the room that suffocated me into silence. My earthly vision of a white room in education is that of peace, equality, and solidarity. I am tired of the all too familiar reminders of being lynched (literally and figuratively) by the majority.

Although I missed my time in the classroom, moving up in education was now a career goal. This new goal was not always the path I desired, but the seed was planted. I was determined and eager to take this new journey. Future plans, goals and careers were rarely discussed in my house, nor do I recall having these discussions with my high school counselor, whoever that was.

This new journey did not always feel pleasant. I remember frequently having to ask myself if I was being envied or slighted by the other Black teachers. Not because of the position, but because I did my job. When it came to consequences, I did not discriminate. My new job was to be firm, fair and consistent. I felt despised more by Black or minority parents. They often fell victim to societal views. Attacking and knocking one another down or back. They assumed that "I believed I was better than them". Are they serious, I would often ask myself? They were obviously ignorant of the struggles I faced for even being in that position. Despite their ludicrous irrational thinking, I ensured that I remained loyal to my calling... I was [a consummate professional]. My mentor, mother in Christ, Vivian Lee reminded me to always remain firm, fair, and friendly, but never familiar. She brought confirmation to what I was expected to do.

As a disciplinarian, I never felt as if I discriminated or displayed favoritism. I prided myself on being equal across the board with all students and staff members. I must admit, my new role was a balancing act. You know the one where Blacks have to remain true to "our people" and loyal to "them" so that we can at least feel slightly equal [and maintain our sanity]. But really, what does that mean or how should that look?

In today's world, this balancing act we face has been titled "codeswitching". Most scholars would say it's how we differentiate in our encounters between whites and Blacks. I despise the balancing act to this day because there's nothing fair or equal about it, talk about "No Justice NO DAMN PEACE!"

Nevertheless, I was in a different kind of white room, one that required me to triple cross my Ts and dot every I, e-v-e-r-y single time. In the eyes of those I left behind in the classroom, I was a female version of "Uncle Tom" on the plantation. Was *that* statement ever made directly to me? Absolutely not, but that's how I felt.

The stares and whispers never went unnoticed. I recall having a younger, Black female teacher tell me that "people think you're mean", with no explanation—she failed to mention that she was "people". The attacks from within your own race are always the most difficult to accept. To this day, this teacher has never explained what she meant; however, this was after a subpar evaluation she received that I was willing to redo. This was new to me because I never expected Black people (those who shared my plight) to be so volatile towards me. I was fair; therefore, I was equal... at least this is what I presumed.

As a dean, with the use of the county's code of conduct book and school's policy, my job consisted of determining the consequence as well as the length of individual suspensions according to progression and severity.

I tried to "work" with students who looked like me, unfortunately, my kindness would often backfire on me. Their parents called, cursing and screaming on the phone because they felt their child's consequence was unfair. I recall, one parent received a trespassing order because she and her husband wanted to "beat my ass" for their daughter's inappropriate and disrespectful behaviors. Oftentimes, I felt hated! I endured too many hits from my own people. I knew my administrators trusted and respected my work ethic; however, I felt less than, although I was in a position that should have allowed me to make a difference. They took every opportunity to remind me that most of my complaints came from "my people".

My professionalism and integrity were often questioned because parents frequently complained to the district (a lynch mob in reverse). For years, I suffered from being trolled on social media. This scrutiny came from those in my community because most white people could care less about me. They knew nothing about an arrest that I had been cleared of. I was hated and disrespected for doing my job as a Dean. Regrettably, they helped to tighten the noose that loosely dangled on my neck.

As much as I desired to make a difference, I was only seen as different. Somehow, I was the problem and not a factor in the solution. The authority of my position was manipulated by ideas of a false sense of loyalty to "our people." I tried to close the gap, instead it seemingly widened! However, I understood I had to maintain total fairness because education requires total equality. Education must be leveled/equal… no one should be made to feel greater than or less than.

Take the Noose Off Challenge: A noose requires lifted suspension from the ground in order to be effective. Too many people within education are actively lynching students and their colleagues. Black and brown people are frequently broken down to the lowest common denominators of life. Seemingly, we always find the strength to rise above it all.

Action: I challenge YOU, my readers, to STOP stifling and choking the life out of students and colleagues with callous actions. W.E.B. Dubois said it best, *"There is no force equal to an individual determined to rise."*

Chapter 3

Life Tests within Public Education

A child cannot be taught by anyone that despises him.
~James Baldwin

When I started middle school in 1987, I transferred from Howard Middle School [a predominantly Black school] to Osceola Middle School [a predominantly white school]. Howard was like home. Nestled in the Black neighborhood as most would define it. My identity mattered to the students and staff members that looked and sounded like me; however, we did have a white principal. Osceola was quite different, considered elite, as it still is today. Not many of my kind are wanted there… We are often considered troublemakers by the majority.

Although I made friends fairly quick, I definitely could tell I was in the minority. The teachers were pleasant, from what I can remember, but no one stood out like Mrs. Earnest, my seventh-grade teacher. Her military background made her a no-nonsense teacher.

One of my friends, Lisa, frequently mocked Mrs. Earnest's response to our misbehavior. She'd fold her arms, tap her foot, hold her head up high in the air all while shaking her finger as she addressed our class. Despite her stern corrections, we knew Mrs. Earnest cared. Her love was evident in her teaching and the way she corrected and disciplined us.

She is still in the classroom at a predominantly Black school today, teaching students with compassion, understanding that many are all fragile. Whenever she sees me, she never fails to ask how things are going for both me and my family. Not all white people use their privilege to keep others oppressed.

My eighth-grade year was not as memorable. However, I do have fond memories of some of the Black staff members, like Mrs. Kiner, Mrs. Boston, Mrs. Brown, and Mrs. Washington. I am a firm believer that children connect with people they can identify with. Therefore, it's crucial to have Black (minority) representation within education, not just within the classroom, but in administrative roles as well.

Mrs. Kiner is still employed at the county office in Employment Services. Mrs. Boston recently retired from being the Title I Director. I believe Mrs. Brown (Business Teacher) retired some years back. I have not seen her in years. Mrs. Washington was our school librarian (she has since passed). These ladies exemplified what Black Excellence should be and look like for young teen girls, no matter what walk of life they experienced.

As a Black teenage girl who grew up in the projects, their presence resonated with me in a manner that lasted a lifetime. Their professionalism and mannerisms were nothing like society wanted me to believe. They were sophisticated, articulate, soft spoken and well dressed. Through them, I saw what I could become. Although they didn't know it, the seeds they planted blossomed at the most opportune times in my life.

Mrs. Earnest planted a seed that taught me to command respect in the classroom. She was both firm and fair and remained unbothered by distractions from certain students. Mrs. Brown planted a seed that not only commanded respect but gave respect in return. She was beautiful, soft spoken, but her ability to command the room was gracefully undeniable. She was wise and cautious in her ways… everything she did was an expression of her love and compassion. Mrs. Kiner, clerk generalist at the time, planted a special seed that helped me to utilize sagacity. She often reminded me that I did not need to address every problem that came up. Sometimes my silence would be enough.

Recently, Mrs. Kiner and I conversed over the phone, and I asked her to recount what she remembered about me. She kindly stated, "You were always pleasant, nice, and well-mannered— It was a joy to see you coming! But you didn't play."

Now, I can't go down memory lane without mentioning Mrs. Boston. She planted seeds of resilience and determination. I equate her rise to Drake's song, "Started from the Bottom." Her journey from a TAII to TAIII (current day paraprofessional), dean, assistant principal, and then principal, followed by retiring from director of federal programs (in Horse Capital of the World), epitomized Black excellence. She was Black Girl Magic before it was coined a hashtag. She recalled me being quiet and reserved. I can concur on the "reserved," but quiet is questionable.

I marvel at a recent conversation she and I had. To sit at her feet ``figuratively", to glean information from her educational journey and her plight through the reigns is truly remarkable. I will cherish these words from her… "I was not going to allow people to make me feel bad about my accomplishments."

Mrs. Washington showed such poise and confidence as she walked the campus providing motherly advice when needed. She was always eager to help while in the library. I remember her living in a nice house with a nicely manicured yard on Jones' side as we called it. She was a pillar in the community, later having the Barbara Washington Center built in her honor.

Transitioning to high school proved to be a pivotal point in my life. I had big dreams to play basketball and run track at the collegiate level. I participated in one season of basketball, then I had to forfeit being on the track team because I got pregnant.

I was 14-years-old (a baby, having a baby). Now, I understand how environments lacking structure oftentimes have dire consequences. My mama worked 12-hour days, sometimes seven days a week, to ensure my siblings and I were well taken care of. My grandma, Chadie, sat with us quite often. I respect and appreciate the fact that my mama hustled hard and did what she had to do to keep a roof over our heads and food in the pantry. My daddy was out of the picture (he still is). He left so he could live a better life, supposedly. Either way, this meant I had a ton of unsupervised free time, no enforced boundaries, and a less structured daily routine. Now that I'm older, I often wonder how a structured life would have played out for me. If things were structured, I may not have given birth to my ROCK, my firstborn, Eddie Quataz ROCKer. His birth gave me the mental push needed to fight on.

 I met the father of my oldest son [Eddie], through one of my best friends. At the time, she dated his older brother. Eddie's dad showed me what I thought love was supposed to be. He whispered sweet nothings (bullshit) in my ear as my grandma would say. Nonetheless, to me his words were comforting, seductive, and proved that I could keep the attention of a young man. Most young girls like me at the time, desired the attention of a young man, a father figure, but would get it from others because our fathers were absent.

It wasn't long before my mama noticed changes in my body and eating habits. I was too naive to know what was going on, but she did. She had been a teen mom herself. We never had "the talk" about how these things happened. I believe we never talked about the "birds and the bees" in an effort to avoid what could and would eventually happen.

Mama was extremely disappointed! She told me, "being "fast" will always catch up with you!" And it did! Getting pregnant wasn't something that I set out to do; sex was simply something to do, and my decision to have unprotected sex changed the trajectory of my life, fortunately in a good way as seasons changed. This was the uncharted path that I now had to take.

It was difficult staying focused while participating in extracurricular activities. I thought being a teen mom would take me out, literally. My daddy wanted me to have an abortion, but I disagreed.

According to statistics, the reckless decision I made was like placing a noose on the neck of my future. Teen Pregnancy

Prevention reports that 3 of 10 American girls will get pregnant at least once before they turn 20. In addition to that, a Huff Post article states that more than 50 percent of teen mothers never graduate high school. Apparently, I was doomed to hang myself and become society's version of a "welfare queen".

The odds were stacked against me; however, I was designed to overcome this major but temporary setback! Even if I was the culprit of my downfall. I eventually learned to dig myself out of my mess, no self-loathing or self-pity… Just determination to be more than my circumstances dictated. It wasn't until I became a teen mom that I realized my son Eddie put a different kind of fight and zeal inside of me. One of my goals was to prove my family members and naysayers wrong. My circumstances would not define me or my son.

My best friends went to a school specifically for teen moms. However, I waddled in the halls of Forest High School because my mama insisted that I continued my education right there. Recently, I asked her why she did not allow me to attend the Phoenix Center, but she pretended as if she never knew that was an option. Most of my teachers, from what I remember, treated me as if I were a typical student. I cannot remember them ever asking how I felt or attempting to connect with me beyond my academics. My pregnancy didn't influence the way they instructed me or their expectations of me at all. Life continued to progress although I was in a place of uncertainty. That dark place of uncertainty felt like being in a science fiction time warp.

After giving birth to Eddie on April 14, 1991, I had to remain home for some time. Mrs. Neasman, a Home Economics teacher at Forest, was assigned to be my homebound teacher. At the time, we were living with my grandmother in a subdivision called Happiness Homes.

Mrs. Neasman visited the house on a weekly basis. She was very sweet and kind to me. She, too, was soft spoken, but did not hold back on how she felt about certain topics. Ms. Neasman never judged me, just provided encouragement and assistance along the way. There were times she would hold my baby while I tended to my schoolwork. There were also times she would take a quick nap or watch Oprah with my granny. Mrs. Neasman was one of us—family. She was welcomed and provided me with the educational services I needed at home so that I could enter back on campus without being behind in my studies.

Students know when teachers care. Mrs. Neasman was one of those teachers. We didn't have much contact after that because I transferred to Vanguard High. I know she passed due to illness some years later. Thank you, Ms. Neasman, for loosening the noose...

Vanguard High was another experience. I remember my honors English teacher, Ms. O'Hara, a thin, young white lady—boy was she tough! That toughness now would be summed up to having high expectations for her students. Needless to say, I dropped her class because I did not want to work that hard. As I look back, no one intervened or asked why I chose to drop her class. I now understand that students need CHAMPIONS to reassure them when hopelessness or doubt arises.

Then there was Ms. Myhand, an older heavy set white lady, who taught liberal arts. She was nice but talked fast. I opted for her class to stay away from trigonometry. No one ever tried to steer me differently. I have no memories at all of my guidance counselor(s). However, I do remember being on track to graduate early and oh boy did that come in handy.

Remediation

You would think I learned my lesson from having unprotected sex with the first son, but I didn't. I guess I needed remediation. I tightened the noose on my own neck again. Here, I met the love of my life, my high school sweetheart, and now HUSBAND. Mr. Jamie D. Gilmore, Sr. We courted, became intimate and not long after welcomed Jamie, Jr. on September 3, 1993, during my junior year of high school. Remember, the statistics I mentioned earlier? Two babies before the age of 20 and still in high school. How could I be so naive and stupid? A second go around and I still do not recall any counselors counseling me on next steps. Where was the young parent program I so desperately needed?

I had no one to bail me out. My mama was completely done this time! She said to me, "You make your bed hard; you lay in it!" She vowed not to attend any appointments or offer any support. Fortunately, she and my grandma Chadie showed up at labor and delivery when it was time for Jamie to make his debut.

Prior to giving birth, I spent 30 days in the hospital due to health complications. Mama and other family members stepped in and took care of Eddie. As I look back over my life now, I see a traumatized young lady determined to navigate the unexpected hand life dealt.

Welfare seemed more promising, but I refused to succumb to a life of monthly handouts or drop out of school. I was close to graduating and ahead of my class. I was educated, book smart but did not have the wherewithal to stay focused with everything going on. Surprisingly, I managed to stay on track and wobble across the stage a year early and received my high school diploma.

Take the Noose Off Challenge: Don't allow past mistakes or the mistreatment of others to determine or dictate your future successes. Perseverance is the ultimate precursor to success. Trust that your journey is purposeful even with the thorns (negatives of life), buds (potential lies within), and the roses (success, light, positivity)!

Action: I challenge you to BELIEVE that you can endure and successfully progress through your journey… no matter what!

Chapter 4

Educational Freedom: College Bound

You're important in your own right. People need to value you because of who you are, because of your story, because of your challenges. That's what makes you unique. ~Michelle Obama

Central Florida Community College (CFCC) was my next stop. At the time, I desired to be a nurse. So, with little to no guidance, I enrolled myself in school as a medical secretary. This was my ticket; I was on my way out. I had no idea this degree was far from what I needed to become a nurse, but this was the path taken. If only I had received wise counsel from my Guidance Counselor, the time spent could have been given to my desired major.

Thankfully, the degree afforded me the opportunity to work at several doctor's offices. I knew I wanted more, so I went back and enrolled in the licensed practical nursing program at CFCC. I was a young unwed mom of two living like I was married but working, partying, and trying to finish school. The balancing act was real.

I participated in study groups, studied alone, excelled in the lab but struggled on the exams. My professors at the time were all white females and didn't seem to care. I was in college now, so I knew the caring and compassionate part of teaching was out the door. Yet, I never gave up.

Unfortunately, I did not make the grade during my first round. My average was 74.6 percent, and I needed a 75 percent; no rounding included, to continue in the program. I was consoled by several of my white classmates, making statements like, "I can't believe you did not make it" or "There was no way we (some of my white classmates) should have made it, and not you."

I believed them, but the writing was on the wall or the paper to be politically correct. I was devastated. I bottled up my pride and resumed working full-time at the doctor's office knowing that I was not ready to quit. I re-entered the LPN program months later but did not have the same passion. It was another failed attempt.

The little engine in me was low on fuel; mentally, physically, and emotionally, but I was determined to not give up. I turned to my boys and asked, "What do y'all think I should do?" They answered with one resounding word, "Teach!" Teaching was not on my repertoire of assignments. Thankfully, my young, intelligent, Black sons (Eddie and Jamie, Jr.) had been given a glimpse into my future (Jeremiah 29:11)! God allowed them to see what I couldn't or what I did not want to see.

Back to school I went, this time to major in Elementary Education. Although I was often teased by my family member as being a lifetime student, I remained at CFCC to complete my Associate of Arts degree. Then, I transferred to Saint Leo University to earn a Bachelor's degree. I was insistent on not allowing history to repeat itself, facing some of the same struggles I witnessed by so many in my family.

On November 11, 2000, I married the love of my life and he encouraged me to complete my college degree. Fall 2001, I was pregnant with our third son and again, I waddled across the stage during commencement. With much purpose, hard work, determination, and intent, we did it!

The Final Exam

It's often said that life is our greatest teacher, and it is! It's also said, it is during adversity that we find out who we really are, and we do! After being in the classroom for almost 10 years, I was hanging on by a thread. Then out of the blue, my family was dealt an emotional blow.

In 2008, my husband had an affair that threw me into a tailspin. Suddenly, time stood still! I couldn't breathe, sleep, or eat. I felt like I was being lynched and MY life was the culprit. The Christian family life and ministry we worked so hard to build was crumbling right before my eyes and I felt hopeless; especially as a pastor's wife.

I was supposed to support my husband and the vision God had given him. However, because the affair was public; I could not do any damage control. I felt powerless. The word was on the streets, and standing in front of students was one of the hardest things I had to do. Some of their parents knew me and they discussed my personal affairs way too much!

With God's strength, I refused to quit on my students, although I was slowly dying inside. I knew how to command my classroom, but my family needed me more. The school where I worked was in jeopardy of being closed down by the state. Everything seemed to be falling apart around me. Life as I knew it changed and it changed us.

I was falsely accused by my husband's mistress of stalking and wrongfully arrested, but ultimately cleared of all charges. Unfortunately, this closed legal case has continued to resurface at some of the most inopportune times. On numerous occasions, parents and students used the situation to attack my character and credibility. I must admit, this situation has brought me to tears, yet I still rise, hold my head up (high), and refuse to be defined by a personal pain turned public; especially at the hands of teenage children trolling me on social media.

Then in 2009, the Superintendent of schools made a political decision to release all teachers from Evergreen Elementary. Teachers were dispersed to all ends of the county. The paraprofessionals were allowed to remain at the school. The school remained open and received an "A" grade.

After the dust settled and prior to relocating to a new school, I needed a break, something different. The pressure was unnerving. I was on an emotional roller coaster, but again refused to quit or give in. My husband and I mended our marriage (privately); it was difficult, but we did it with the help of the Lord. My husband and I were transparent about the arrest, counseling and everything that turned our lives into crumbles. Our sons learned valuable life lessons, such as supporting each other and remaining focused in school despite the circulating rumors.

As others laughed and pointed fingers, family members squawked and called me a lifetime student, I kept pushing. I yearned for something different. I decided to take a year off from public education and go back to nursing school at CFCC in 2009, but this time I'd attempt the RN program. I felt like I needed to retreat from the chaos and escape from the public spotlight.

I was destined to defy the odds. I've learned that whatever doesn't break us, definitely builds us. The exams of our lives make us stronger than we'll ever know.

Take the Noose Off Challenge: Directives to withstand the noise of the white rooms.

P - Persevere through mistreatment, demand to be heard, and refuse to be lynched in your silence.

U - Understand that the purpose of this plight is greater than personal attacks.

S - Stay focused as you seek spaces and rooms that welcome, appreciate, and value you!

H - Have a plan, pursue your purpose, and perpetuate lucrative actions.

Chapter 5

The Struggle within My Calling

I raise up my voice-not so I can shout, but so that those without a voice can be heard…we cannot succeed when half of us are held back
~Malala Yousafzai

I've always had an innate yearning to help others, no matter what that "help" looked like. As a professional educator, I understand I am also a lifetime learner. Consequently, I've come to realize that my calling (educating, helping, liberating - it's all the same), is also the reason I struggle with remaining committed. I've seen too many inequalities, experienced too many inequalities, and yet I'm constantly told I'm too much, but I am treated like I will never be enough!

Trauma in the school and workplace is an everyday reality for Black and brown adults and children, but our pain is dismissed because we are expected to be strong, regardless. What does it mean to be strong… for us? Black and brown individuals don't exemplify strength because we want to, our strength is pertinent to our survival in every capacity of life, most notably in the white rooms. Those suffocating rooms that attempt to squeeze the life out of you like a python wrapped around its prey.

At times, teaching drained life out of me, physically, mentally, and emotionally. The educational politics that govern our public schools and strip educators of their liberty to simply teach are stifling. Racially and politically biased school boards and incompetent district staff are the primary culprits of educational lynching!

Undeniably, these factors tightened the noose around education. Now, the state of education is one of the primary weapons used to further ostracize Black and brown students and educators.

Standardized Assessments Are Lynching Us

In the book "Smoke and Mirrors," author Dan Baum detailed his interview with President Nixon's chief of staff, H.R. Haldeman, who quoted Nixon as saying, "You have to face the fact that the whole problem is really the Blacks. The key is to devise a system that recognizes this while not appearing to." This statement was made in the 1970s. This was reauthorized by Presidents Regan (1980s), Clinton (1990s) and George W. Bush (2000s). This noose was called No Child Left Behind (aka the death of purposeful education). Blacks were never expected to thrive or survive in a world that was literally built on the back of its people.

Standardized testing is a system of implicit bias, and it further perpetuates the practice of educational exclusion instead of inclusion. They have been utilized since the early 1800s. The Army alpha and Beta tests (multiple choice), developed during World War I to sort soldiers by their mental abilities, became a model for schools. According to the FDOE website, in 1998 the FCAT "was designed to measure achievement of the Sunshine State Standards." Moreover, the stated primary goal of these assessments is to "provide information needed to improve the public schools by enhancing the learning gains of all students and to inform parents of the educational progress of their public-school children."

From the Public Education Classroom to the Penitentiary:

At the innocent age of nine years old, third grade students are tracked to prison.

Their annual reading assessment tests are required for promotion to fourth-grade. This is also oppression because teachers are now teaching to a test versus providing a diverse learning experience for all students. Unfortunately, education continues to be racially constricting. The noose is still there because racial hierarchy takes precedence over educational equality.

I can recall my first years of teaching at a predominantly Black school, it was recently closed by the state. My students were often labeled as having behavioral issues and some at times performed poorly on standardized testing. The very testing that should have been used to guide instruction and provide personalized interventions was now being used to punish students by retaining them due to substandard performance.

My students were used to being berated, belittled, and often dismissed by those who chose to teach them. Undoubtedly, prior to becoming a certified professional educator, most teachers complete four-years of pedagogical studies. Teaching is the practice of elevating while embracing individual uniqueness! Unfortunately, within the American educational system, too many students are constantly oppressed by those who teach them.

Seemingly, the students I taught were the posterchildren for the school to prison pipeline, because clearly, they would end up in jail or dead… right? The modern-day lynching tree has several nooses… the American education system is just one of them. This is the fate of too many students when they are seen from the lenses of their oppressors. Seeing is always believing The oppressor doesn't hear the student asking a question because they're genuinely confused. The oppressor says the student is being belligerent, writes him up, and refuses to teach him.

I witnessed this recently, during a random walkthrough. I entered an Intensive Reading classroom, and the teacher was leaning against her desk. The students looked at me and said, "Mrs. Gilmore, she said she's not teaching us." I was appalled, but not surprised. This teacher has made it quite evident that she does not want or like teaching intensive reading; and she has no desire to teach these students (most of them are Black).

I intervened and addressed the students directly. I didn't use any flowery euphemisms; I needed my words to resonate with them. Most of these students were placed in her class because of low test scores. I told them they would remain in this class if they chose not to do the work. As I spoke, another student interjected and said, "She don't like us." I responded, "That may be true, but you're still responsible for doing the work.

Teachers don't like some of their students and vice versa. This is a fact. To be honest, many teachers are there for consistent income and insurance benefits. They show up daily {unenthused] and they add more misery and pressure to students who are already at a disadvantage. The belief is that schools will not receive any acceleration points, achievement points for certain students, so why bother teaching them. Too often, generalizations of this kind are stated as facts and they manifest as realities. Florida's educational system has evolved to a system that values points over students and sound education. Some international studies have even indicated that U.S. schools were among the world's most segregated and inequitable.

Although it has been an arduous task to reshape our students' minds to believe they can and will excel... We did it! Over a period of five consecutive school terms, our faculty intentionally implemented the practice of truly caring! We built relationships with our students because they mattered, and we wanted them to know that. We conducted sporadic home visits, celebrated their improvements, and taught our students to see their mistakes as an opportunity to learn - and not failure! I have always treated my students like my children. I am firm, fair, and ensure that boundaries are established and maintained.

One student in particular, CJ, had a lengthy behavior record and poor grades. He was high risk due to scoring a level one on FCAT toppled with class grades and behavior. Having two sons at the time, I viewed him as another. I knew he had potential and worked hard to prove it to him. It was not an easy task, but I set high expectations, held him accountable and loved him along the way. I was also not afraid to involve his parents. Many times, Black parents are left out because white teachers feel threatened by them and fail to include them in the educational journey. CJ managed to bring his grades up, his behavior improved, and he passed the FCAT that year with a level 3. It was my job not only to educate him but to be willing to see him as a person. He went on and successfully finished elementary, middle, and high school. He also thrived in sports. He beat the odds that were set against him.

JT, another student, did not have the same success story. He too had poor grades and behavior. His family was known for matriculating through that school with little to no success, unfortunately for him, he was doomed the moment he stepped on that campus. He never achieved level 3 on FCAT, but both his behavior and grades improved. His smile could light up the room.

JT managed to finish elementary school, middle and high too, but faced run-ins with law enforcement. He has been in and out of jail since. His path was painstakingly painted for him at a very young age. The system that manages to make money off the backs of our students had failed him.

I Do My Job!

As an administrator, students are my primary concern. I often remind teachers and tell students that our main goal is to get them to school and home safely. This does not minimize the importance of teachers or instruction; however, school safety is a national issue that makes headlines daily. Therefore, creating and maintaining an environment that is safe and conducive for learning, classroom management and discipline are paramount.

However, I experienced the most frustration when I interacted with white students, especially the female students. Their parents claimed my pedagogical approach was "too harsh" but the parents of most Black students appreciated my teaching style. In all honesty, many times it boiled down to race although most love to say, I don't see color, a statement of cowardice. That would be a chapter all by itself.

Respect is and will always be KEY! I do not expect any child to be perfect, but respect is mandatory. Consequently, my classes were extremely structured and regimented; I set high expectations for all my students, and I expected them to meet or exceed them.

This never seemed to be a problem with administration when they wanted to place a problematic student in my class. For some reason, Caucasian teachers holding the same degree as African American teachers seemed to lack disciplinary acumen, especially with Black and Brown students, thus causing them to shed their white tears all the while requesting targeted students to be removed from their class.

Without hesitation Black teachers are deemed the miracle workers of disciplinary action. We're too mean to some and just right for others. Quite frequently, white teachers would send their students to one of our classrooms (usually with an administrator's approval). We manage, but it is not our plight to be the universal disciplinarian.

I can vividly recall one occasion where my Assistant Principal requested that I allow an unruly student in my classroom. I refused and told her the teacher in question possessed a degree in education just like me. Therefore, it was not my job to manage her class and mine; this teacher obviously needed some professional development in classroom management.

On the other hand, if a Caucasian parent thought we were "too strict," not educated enough, or lacked compassion, they would request for their child to be placed in a nicer (white) teacher's class. Utter nonsense if I must say. Now please do not misunderstand me. I have dealt with my fair share of African American parents who thought I was targeting their child, or I did not like their child. Parents, despite race or ethnicity, fail to realize that the problem was never the child, but the child's behavior or academic performance.

According to the American Psychological Association (APA), classroom management is the process by which teachers and schools create and maintain appropriate behavior of students in classroom settings. The purpose of implementing classroom management strategies is to enhance prosocial behavior and increase student academic engagement (Emmer & Sabornie, 2015; Everston & Weinstein, 2006). Good classroom management often provides the structure needed to maintain safety and an environment conducive for learning. Students need boundaries, rules, and accountability.

Today, many teachers struggle with providing structure and safe learning environments, and it's not because they're incapable of managing their classroom, but they simply choose to ignore certain behaviors while noticeably reprimanding others. Furthermore, some teachers are in denial when it comes to dealing with their own biases— implicit and explicit.

One of the most problematic issues is the use of cell phones in the classroom and on campuses. The code of conduct for the county states that cell phones should not be visible or activated. Yes, they can be used for instructional purposes, but most are not. They are often used to pacify behaviors or befriend students.

I once worked at a high school where on any given day, you could walk into a classroom and students were on Instagram, TikTok or Facetiming their friend or even sometimes a parent. It was evident the principal, a former superintendent's daughter, was okay with this behavior on her campus because it was happening in multiple classes on a daily basis. Students were not trying to be discrete. In fact, this principal's daughter was a senior at the school, so to me the principal who's still at this very school today, had to maintain an image that was pleasing to her daughter and her daughter's peers.

Take the Noose Off Challenge: Practice being F.A.I.R.

Factual - Unbiased practices within education and the benefit of it.

Acknowledgement - We deserve a free quality public education.

Inclusive - Education should include the experiences of all educators, students, and parents. Educational bias is not a minority issue… It is an issue of historical oppression and institutionalized racism used to keep Black and brown people subjugated.

Representation – Without relativity within education, comprehension is nearly impossible.

Action: - Excellence is a mindset that is maintained through the habitual practice of accountability, fairness, compassion, integrity, respect, and transparency that makes us all equal.

I challenge you [whether you work in education or not] to practice being fair! It is the golden rule… "Treat others the way you want to be treated."

Chapter 6

Reading, wRiting, aRithmetic & Racism

*The chief objective of education is NOT to learn things,
but to Unlearn things ~Gilbert Chesterton*

Through the years, education has experienced its fair share of turnover and turmoil. Some will agree that it has become a political nightmare for students, educators, and parents. Growing up, I cannot recall a time when my mama ever worried about my siblings, and I being retained due to testing. However, things changed as I evolved into parenthood.

In 1996, the Sunshine State Standards were adopted. They were initially or reportedly developed to assist with increasing student growth. This ultimately meant that expectations would be raised for student learning and that learning would be assessed by uniformed standards based on a standardized test. I couldn't help but wonder if this was a strategic plan of the majority to keep our people down. Too often I feel as if we are being set up and setback.

One must never forget the trick of the enemy. Remember how slaves were forbidden to read and write, because reading equated to knowledge (but more importantly power), which led to liberation mentally and physically. This is why it could have cost them their lives for reading.

In March 2021, Florida Governor Ron DeSantis declared that teaching critical race theory teaches students to hate their country and to hate each other and it is not worth one red cent. However, I must offer the wise words of Maya Angelou: *``The more you know of your history, the more liberated you are''*. DeSantis, why do you feel your history is more important than mine? Is it because you fear that we will rise up and become more educated and developed as a people? In this great country of the U.S.A, some 400 years later, we are still yelling, "Let My People Go!"

We cannot continue to ignore history, the lack of diversity, and the need to implement change in public education. Likened to a construction zone, we must start from the ground up, build trusting relationships with all students, parents, and administration [regardless of race, gender, socio-economic status]. This work isn't for the fainthearted because change is work. It requires unlearning, relearning, and reimagining a fresh vision for equitable education.

In order to rectify these inequities, those working within public education must be committed to the success of every student. Although teachers and administrators serve on the front lines of education, guidance counselors play a significant role in ensuring student achievement.

According to learn.org, the role of guidance counselors is to work with students and parents to help guide students' academic, behavioral, and social growth. Unfortunately, most students don't even know who their school counselors are. Unsurprisingly, I cannot recall the names of my guidance counselors either. Since I was a teenage mother, I needed all the guidance I could get. I guess my counselor predetermined that I was a lost cause.

I asked my husband and three sons, "Do any of you remember your high school guidance counselors?" My husband had no recollection. My oldest son, who graduated in 2009 stated that he vaguely remembered his. My middle son who graduated in 2012 could not remember either, but the youngest, who graduated in 2020 did recall his counselors.

My youngest son had a Hispanic counselor who was more visible and accessible because he coached sports. The other female Hispanic counselor assisted in correcting an Algebra course (9th grade) that somehow got overlooked in his middle school years. She was amazing!

High school is one of the most significant educational experiences in a child's life. They need a support system that truly desires to cultivate the best for them. This requires intentional effort to do more than the usual... Don't sit behind the desk and do nothing, don't be selective and cater to the "good" students while ignoring and criticizing others. Without consistent and caring guidance, the most vulnerable students continue to lack, especially in education. Ignorance *cannot* be bliss if education is power.

Take the Noose Off Challenge: Practice C.A.R.E.

Consistency - Consistently do what's right by all students.

Accountability - Be accountable for your actions and how they affect all students.

Revitalize - Enhance educational practices that are equitable for all students.

Empower - Create systems and strategies that enhance learning for all students.

Chapter 7

Appointed the New House ~~Nigger~~ Administrator

If you're silent about your pain, they'll kill you and say you enjoyed it
~Zora Neale Hurston

When I first became a dean, I was equipped with classroom management skills. However, the learning curve as a quasi-administrator was sharp because dealing with adults, politics and district policies were often challenging to say the least. Adults alone are taxing because we "think" we have all the answers; therefore, we hear, but we don't listen. Politically, education has been placed in the hands of financial stakeholders rather than those who genuinely care. Lastly, district policies are supposed to be student-centered, unfortunately, many of these policies are overshadowed by the feelings of the policy makers and parents (with their own personal agendas).

Discipline has always been considered to be the "best fit" position for African Americans in the public school system. An excerpt from an African American male teacher in the Philadelphia Inquirer made such a profound statement, "Black teachers are expected to be disciplinarians of Black children, have talks about the need to code-switch, and be experts on all things racism and diversity for Black students and white teachers." This is not what we desire, but what most white administrators and/or our colleagues believe we're master disciplinarians on the Education Plantation. Why is that? Are we only capable of correcting behaviors and not transforming mindsets and improving learning outcomes? Applied knowledge is power; however, the room that we are often kept in is suffocating. We, African American women, are often viewed as either too opinionated or too angry when using our "voice", even in positions that require our voices to be heard, respected, and valued!

Historically, Black women have been dehumanized, treated unethically, raped, and forced to silence; yet the house-nigger maintained order. This meant rearing white children, literally feeding them from the breast, doing chores and pleasing the slave master. No matter the abuse they endured, silence and loyalty to the slave master was expected.

Sadly, we still face the same hardships within the Education Plantation. We are euphemistically silenced and told to be content while serving in low-level leadership roles [although we are just as qualified as our white counterparts]. Somehow, we've transitioned from the master's house to maintaining order in the school house; yet we are expected to be token representatives of our race.

Our authority is minimized when we speak up and out against the status quo. We are accused of being aggressive, difficult, angry, rude, and unprofessional when we simply voice the truth. By no means am I power stricken; however, I respect the chain of command in my school district. I play by the rules because I have to— white privilege doesn't save us, it never has. Policies become our comfort and our keepers. What's in Black and white is all we have if we're going to have any level of accountability.

The Unmitigated Gall of White People

"Just be patient, your time is coming." Easy for them to say, when it's always been their time and their turn. I've heard this statement several times, usually from my white peers. It is the equivalent of slaves being free but remaining on the plantation because it's all they know. My promotion was deserved but the blatant dismissal of my presence and authority was cruel and undeserved.

Likened to the presidency, Black and brown women wait eagerly every four years for the new school superintendent to be elected, praying that a change will come. Surely, we have arrived with the newly appointed Superintendent. To the dismay of many, like the stillness in the night air, we still wait. My plight, our plight, can never be understood by those who have not walked in my shoes. Unsurprisingly, many of my white counterparts audaciously believe that my presence here "in this position" should be questioned, taken, or never been granted.

In 2003, Ocala Star Banner published an updated article on desegregation previously published in 1968. The article titled, "Fight to desegregate school system continues" addressed similar situations we are still plagued with today. Many minorities had been overlooked or kept in a lower position only to train their equal who would eventually become their principal. The past will always resurface, unless we are willing to face it head on. School board attorney at that time, John McKeever, stated "desegregation is something that "if you don't keep it in front of you, it's easy to forget". One can only assume that's why so many school board officials in America are suffering from amnesia.

How much longer must we wait? I couldn't help but think time was indeed passing me by. African Americans have been waiting and proving we deserve to lead, be heard, and acknowledged. Hell, we've been waiting and fighting for equal rights since we were forced to assimilate into the United States of America. We are tired

I was promoted to Assistant Principal on July 18, 2019. Within my position, I was responsible for maintaining disciplinary balance and evaluating teacher performance. Unfortunately, although Black and Brown students are the minority, the majority of students I reprimanded often looked like me. When Black and Brown students make poor choices or are perceived to be disrespectful; I wonder how many of my colleagues actually put forth the effort to provide proper redirection before the student arrives to my office. There always seems to be a sense of rejection before restoration.

The primary duty of any educator is to recognize and cultivate greatness within each student. Rita Pierson stated it best, "Every child deserves a champion: an adult who will never give up on them, who understands the power of connection and insists they become the best they can possibly be." However, this cannot be done when the child is perceived as troubled, unteachable, and unworthy of a quality education.

The public education plantation has failed to expand its reach because there are too many politicians seeking re-election and "financial stakeholders" that are more concerned with (monetary) profits, power, and pleasing people, versus improving students' performance and comprehension or their educational journey.

Students cannot perform satisfactorily when they have issues beyond the walls of their classroom. From school and neighborhood shootings to homelessness, many students cannot comprehend anything outside of their personal problems. It is almost impossible as many students do not have the luxury or access to resources that will enable them to be successful, sometimes resulting from concentrated poverty.

As an administrator, I understand the importance of caring for students [first] and then disciplining them as their "servant-leader." Unfortunately, far too many of our students don't care to listen because they haven't been heard. Therefore, I am intentional about the relationships I establish with my students and their parents. You cannot teach a child until they know you care about them, which requires building trust.

Methods that work must be practiced I believe Restorative disciplinary practices should be implemented within confounds of the classroom. Restorative Practices (RP) is an alternative to exclusionary disciplinary practices; instead, restorative practices repair the harm that's done when a standard of conduct is violated (State of Nevada, DOE). For example, as a dean, students have rolled their eyes or neck at me, but I gave it back to them, literally! However, I also showed them how their actions could be perceived as being disrespectful?

Culturally, our interactions were an expression of acceptance and understanding. We must take time to understand the culture of others. It opens the door for candid conversations and empathy.

As a minority working in Educational Administration, my position satisfies the status quo and keeps the students in line. Too often it has been insinuated, *"You're Black, you understand them better."* This is just one of the implicit biases (stereotypes) faced by Black Americans in education. While other instances are quite explicit.

For example, around the time of the Colin Kaepernick's kneeling controversy… While conversing with a group of my white colleagues, one of them said, "Let's ask Mrs. Gilmore what she thinks about Colin Kaepernick." I wanted to say, "What's the damn problem?" It was in fact his right to express how he felt… freely (freedom of speech, right?). This was such a provocative topic at the time, and I was the only Black person present. Was I expected to fold? Clearly, none of them understood the true meaning behind "taking a knee" and I didn't take issue with it. At that moment, I clearly understood the many nuances of dwelling and working in the "white rooms."

Unconscious, or implicit, biases are the attitudes, preferences, and assumptions individuals hold toward another individual or group of people. These beliefs—whether true or false— cause contention and hinder progress.

Having to exist in a world with such crippled perceptions and biases is extremely burdensome. Yet, many African Americans, like me, enter white rooms daily knowing that our existence, influence, and our position doesn't seem to matter, but it does!

As a professional Black woman within education, I have often felt powerless. Whether I was in the classroom or in an administrative office, I have experienced blatant and subliminal racism, sexism, and classism. ALL of the damn 'ISMs! Although my reality is true and what I experience is factual, I am still demonized and my presence is unappreciated and constantly devalued. When I used my voice, I was told I was too LOUD, too ABRUPT, too HARSH, and too AGGRESSIVE! Now, I sit in a position of "change" but my authority, my expertise, and my rationale are constantly challenged and questioned. This is the plight of being "The House ~~Nigger~~ Administrator" on the Education Plantation.

Take the Noose Off Challenge: Be intentional about ensuring Black and Brown women aren't just assistant principals. We are well qualified to lead in all capacities and grade levels, not just assist. This means there is a critical need and cry for school districts to focus and be deliberate on appointing leaders who represent the student body, beyond stereotypical entry-level positions.

Chapter 8

Pain in Promotion

"There are also women I have never met but who are recorded in the pages of history and whose lives and struggles inspire me and thousands of other working women to keep putting one foot in front of another every day."
~Ketanji Brown Jackson, Supreme Court Justice

Education has drastically shifted over the years. States have become more focused on school grades wherein counties have become fixated on points versus people. Teachers are now more focused on their ratings (highly effective, effective) rather than true student achievement. The overwhelming pressure to maintain exemplary school grades and high student success on standardized testing is educationally stifling.

Students, teachers, schools, and districts have been penalized for poor school grades and granted less funding. This is a perpetuation of misappropriated federal and state dollars on a much larger scale. At the height of the covid pandemic, the right righteous Florida governor threatened to rob schools of funding due to his personal innuendos and insensitivity to mask wearing. This is an example of political foolery and educational lynching at its worst.

The career I loved transformed into a daily battle of simply making it through my work day. I needed a change. So, I applied to various positions in the county. My mind was set on becoming a reading coach. I landed several interviews, and I also received my fair share of canned email responses. Typical responses for most Black and brown individuals (especially Black women) who attempt to better themselves in the great horse capital of the world. Needless to say, I was granted an opportunity to serve as a dean at a middle school.

I was thrilled to start this new phase in my career. Fortunately for me, I was unaware of the heartache and tears it would bring. If I had known I would be "bullied" by students, parents, and staff, trolled on social media, I probably would have opted to either remain in the classroom or seek other career opportunities outside the realms of education.

Although I was welcomed by most of my colleagues, I encountered a young white female dean who seemed quite perturbed by my Black face in this white room. The negative energy she hid behind that smile and blue eyes was quite daunting. She desired to see me fail. Therefore, she intentionally withheld useful information to assist me while transitioning into my new position.

Condescendingly, this same woman laughed at the first referral I processed. A female student cursed me out. I did not fully understand the codes on the infractions (1-4), because I was a novice, I coded this particular incident as a Level 3-gross insubordination. Ms. "No-Help's" laughter at my inexperience was my initiation into the new world of educational discipline. At that moment, I understood the reality of working in the white room and not just being there. Again, I still had to dot every "I" and cross every "T"— every single time. The white room did not allow any errors [for me].

As time went on, I often told myself, I did not sign up for this SHIT! The lack of respect or the disrespect from students, parents and staff was unreal. I was cautious with everything I said and the people I spoke to. I was told to TRUST NO ONE! I felt as if I was nothing more than a slave on the modern-day plantation. Looking over my shoulder, walking on eggshells, trying not to offend my oppressors as I attempted to survive… thriving almost seemed laughable in the white room!

During these moments, I was reminded of a story my mama told me about one of her patients. Her patient, "Mr. Wilson said, "Sometimes you have to laugh to keep from crying." Unsurprisingly, as a Black female administrator my reality is shared with several women and people of color. It is taxing and detrimental to several facets of our lives (health, family, work-relationships, and career).

As the school year progressed, the days got longer and the intensity of misbehaviors magnified. Many days, I was cursed out and threatened by insolent students along with their parents for just doing my job [correcting behaviors to ensure school safety]. There seemed to be no boundaries when the face-to-face threats and calls transpired. No one seemed to have basic respect for human existence, not to mention respect for authority. But yet, I was told many times to listen more, allow them to "vent." Give them a listening ear. I guess it's okay for me to be "BULLIED"!

On countless occasions, I was blatantly disrespected by white and Black parents. My safety was threatened, and my job security was sustained by my ability to remain "in my place", respectfully. I can recall one encounter when a white dad left a voicemail screaming and threatening to harm me if I even looked at his child. This was due to a dress code violation. On a different occasion, a Black mom, also threatened to whoop my ass over a dress code violation. Sadly, I was told to embrace the mantra… "don't take it personal".

Most days I didn't, but the insults stung from time to time, and it has taken everything in me not to retaliate. One thing is certain, you can't reason with unreasonable people. Disrespect is an unspoken rule of engagement inside the white rooms, classrooms, and the campus/school district overall.

I am still striving to effectively do my job while remaining silent simultaneously. The white rooms attempted to silence me while being the puppeteers of my authority. I was given "power" yet I felt powerless. Although I pride myself on being fair and consistent, my integrity was and is constantly questioned. Several Black and brown parents often accused me of "being too white," "throwing my weight around," or "targeting their kids." The white parents demeaned and minimized my authority and expertise. According to many of them, I was too aggressive and lacked the necessary intelligence to hold an administrative position.

Schools are supposed to be safe zones [for everyone - including leaders]. One of my primary job duties was to correct behaviors and encourage students to make positive choices. However, I am questioned or chastised on a regular basis by parents and students about my past instead of focusing on the inappropriate behaviors presented by their children. Unfortunately, safety cannot be guaranteed when parents, students, teachers, and administrators fail to practice it amongst each other.

Even now, acts of violence against teachers/educators are extremely common. Social media has empowered these sickening behaviors. We must face the facts and understand that a lot of these behaviors are sometimes perpetuated by the lack of support from parents. Students are reactive to the environment that surrounds them.

An environment that's safe and conducive to learning for all students means following the rules (code of conduct, classroom expectations) even if you do not agree. If schools were able to spend less time correcting poor behaviors: weapons on campus, drugs, fights, sex, profanity, sagging, dress code violations, cell phones, social media, and parent squabbles, then more time could be used to enhance quality instruction and education.

My experience as an administrator forced me to realize the view from the yard may not always be better than the porch, but at least it gets us closer to the table. Accountability starts at our doorstep. One of my personal vows as an educator is: "to help students; especially minorities, realize the potential that lies within them. Hard work is required, because the forty acres and a mule is in Never-never Land.

Take the Noose Off Challenge: "I DON'T SEE COLOR" - This phrase is often misused and overused by our white counterparts who fail to acknowledge the abusive injustices Black and brown people encounter in schools and workplaces. It comes straight from the pits of HELL.

This challenge requires us to **see color** and not be dismissive of the pain others experience; it's inexcusable. Things are not equal as some may believe. I desire to be seen and heard! Understand me. More importantly, feel me and empathize with the traumatic experiences many Black and brown people face daily.

Chapter 9

All Educated Out: BLACKed Out, Burnt Out, Pushed Out

"…Rarely do we share that even good things can sometimes play out in complicated, painful, and confusing ways. Your biggest promotion can come along with some of your most bewildering blows." ~Elaine Welteroth

During Trump's presidency, a time when our country was facing extreme civil unrest. I received a call from Tom and Karen (former principals) from the district office. In our county, those who have been demoted somehow find a way to secure a better paying job. It pays to be white, no pun intended!

Nevertheless, these two characters called to inform me that they had completed my investigation. I failed to mention that I was placed under investigation due to an unstable paraprofessional, who I had never had an issue with, sent an email to the Superintendent stating that I was bullying her. This was followed by a family member's now wife, who reported me for snatching a child up from the floor by his arms. Anyone that knows me knew these accusations did not match my character.

It was one attack after another, one from the white team the other from the Black team. Unsurprisingly, both investigations turned out to have unsubstantiated claims (not guilty)! However, being cleared of all allegations came with a price.

I now had a target placed on my back. Double jeopardy was now in play. A counseling letter for "TONE" was placed in my file. I was banished from city schools and sent to serve my time in the forest, a place where people have been rumored to be openly expressive with prejudiced behaviors. What some would call Trump Territory! I asked Tom if I could talk it over with my husband before making a choice. He responded in a snarky tone, "That is your choice!" Asshole was the initial thought uttered in my mind, (in my best Viola Davis voice)!

Imagine being banished, sent far east of town, across the bridge, to be an Assistant Principal of Discipline to little white kids whose parents loved Trump. Interpret that however you may! What person with integrity would send a Black lady to a white island in a climate of such intense hate? That was my thought exactly.

One Saturday afternoon, I decided to take the forty-five-minute drive that and I was welcomed by numerous Trump 2020 signs and flags. I thought to myself... *Are they serious, I am Black woman traveling out east, over the bridge, alone in the dark, in Trump territory?* It was frightening (for me) to say the least. I responded by sending an e-mail to the acting Deputy Superintendent at the time, letting him know I felt this was a safety concern for me due to the current climate. Tom, the arrogant asshole, now had to reach back out to me with a choice of the elementary school in the forest or the preppy college (high school) south of town. What I thought was a blessing, turned out to be a curse. I was excited to have an opportunity to work at a high school. I could now check yes to all the experience boxes. Elementary school - check, Middle school - check, High school -check. Little did I know, the nightmare on Becky's street was in full effect.

Becky seemed eager to meet me. We met on a Sunday afternoon after church in late January 2021. She shared a little about herself and her family and I did the same. My initial impression was pleasant. I walked away feeling like I would start afresh. At the time, I had no idea the district had not shared why I was sent there, at least that's what Becky later told me. My title on paper was Assistant Principal of Curriculum (APC) as I was replacing the one who had resigned; however, I was assigned the role of Assistant Principal of Discipline (APD). I had no objection to the position; I was just looking for a fresh start. The freshness became quickly tarnished. It was evident "My Blackness" was not wanted there.

However, I was openly accepted by most of the students, especially the Black ones. The students now had a Black woman, in an administrative position they could relate to. One Black female student commented "It's about time they got some Blackness around here." Her statement validated the fact that I am and was needed! Eighty percent of educators are white females, and 80% of our students are minorities. Representation is a necessity; it inspires greatness that is otherwise left untapped.

Becky's posse showed such disdain towards me. They were angered by my presence and the working environment was extremely frigid. If looks could kill, I would have been dead within the second week of my arrival. I had my own fashion designers, none of whom I would have personally hired. Even to this day, white people feel as if they are obligated to comment on my attire. They almost never follow the golden rule, "If you don't have anything good to say, don't say anything at all." The comments and remarks sometimes cut deep like the thorns from the cotton bushes picked by my ancestors.

They attempted to make themselves seem more superior, regardless of their personal appearance. I believe most of their eyes are concealed with scales preventing them from taking a self-evaluation of the hate and white privilege they possess. They refuse to take the time to know the true intent of our hearts, and they are apprehensive regarding our intellectual capabilities.

The coldness and stillness of the white room had caught up with me; yet again. It was later revealed to me that the resentment was due to others feeling they deserved the position I earned and worked for (Assistant Principal on Assignment). When people say it's lonely at the top, what I felt was an understatement.

I was being dangled from the Empire State building. The strong Black woman was under attack. The hour-long meetings on Mondays were dreadful. All I needed was a straight-jacket. The white room was surreal. It was 10 to 1 on most days. Imagine being the only one in a room surrounded by people who hate your very presence. To my white counterparts, imagine being the only one in a room full of people that don't look like you or relate to you? Take a breath and allow that to sink in.

The mental anguish was so overwhelmingly real, I eventually sought therapy. Until recently, therapy was unthinkable in most Black communities. I was thankful to be in a place where I was being supported by my husband, family members and girlfriends. I refused to continually suffer in silence!

Over the span of three short months in this administrative position, I had several demeaning experiences. Some of them are listed below:

- I was yelled at and embarrassed by a teacher in front of staff and students. She was upset because she felt that I was favoring the Black students with disabilities (ESE), often referred to as "these/those" kids.

- I was yelled at by the football coach, who left his class unattended to take a phone call. The Librarian later stated that this was usual behavior from the coach; however, he was never addressed by administration [to my knowledge].

- I was continuously critiqued openly by a paraprofessional and others about my professional attire.

- I was accused of showing favoritism to a Black student for not suspending her although it was her first offense.

- I was openly reprimanded by Becky in front of other staff members. She would send group emails to keep me in my place.

I went home and cried almost daily, but a Black woman's tears are often discredited. Ruby Hamad's, White Tears/Brown Scars book offers great details on "Strategic White Womanhood," which is a spectacle that permits the actual issue at hand to take a back seat to the emotions of the white woman, with the convenient effect that the status quo continues unabated. White women's tears are fundamental to the success of whiteness. Their distress is a weapon that prevents people of color from being able to assert themselves or to effectively challenge white racism and alter the fundamental inequalities built into the system." White women are often protected and deemed damsels in distress.

I felt as if God was punishing me. Lord, what am I supposed to learn from all of this pain, I often ask? I had not done anything to be treated so unfairly. Possibly, because I am my grandparents' dreams realized. Now, I minutely understand the pain of being "the Black one in the white room- the modern-day plantation." I reached out for help on many occasions. I had no idea the people I reached out to in the district office were Becky's accomplices. One of the Area Directors, Paul, came out to meet with her a few times. I was invited to one of the meetings and again asked for help. If my tone is an issue, how do I correct it?

To this day, I am still waiting for an answer. One of Paul's final visits resulted in me getting another counseling letter for "TONE", the very thing I asked for help to correct. I had worked in this district for over 15 years and had never been counseled for this new buzz word, TONE. The word was out. Leaked by people who were supposed to coach me.

What are my next steps, I asked myself? This time, I sent an email to both the Superintendent and Deputy Superintendent seeking help. I asked for the Superintendent to meet with me alone to avoid information being leaked again, but my request was not granted. She assured me the meeting would be confidential. Being new to the area, she obviously had no idea of the connections district officials shared. This meeting ended with another meeting with me, Becky, and a mediator. That resulted in things going from bad to worse. My hostile work environment became a nightmare. I waved the white flag; unfortunately, it did not help in the white room.

I was fighting a losing battle. I ended up taking a leave of absence to remain sane. I also wanted to avoid having another mugshot. This one would definitely be legit. These white damsels in distress were on my last nerve. Becky was protected. Becky's father was a Superintendent in the county for eight years. Her unprofessional behavior went unchecked. She managed to push me out and hire the white woman she wanted from the very beginning. The Superintendent and Deputy Superintendent were at odds, and they did not offer solace. They were both in a new place where they were hired and could be fired by the school board at any time.

In June 2020, the good ole boy system was slowly being dismantled. For the first time ever, a Superintendent was appointed providing a glimmer of hope; for those who are marginalized or left behind... This is what I believed *at first*.

In its past and current state, I have concluded that MCPS stands for (M)aking (C)olored-minorities (P)eople (S)uffer, both students and staff. Over the years, many minorities continue to share their painful stories of being disrespected, overlooked, demoted, ostracized, and dehumanized in this 21st century.

In my current position as Assistant Principal of Discipline (APD), the buzz word "TONE" has surfaced yet again. I worked for my current principal for four years as a Dean. Prior to receiving my promotion to Assistant Principal, I had never received a negative evaluation. Now, he has also placed "TONE" in my evaluation.

Is this a coincidence? No, this is just reality in MCPS. Numerous Blacks have faced insurmountable attacks on their character, work ethics, and culture from the privileged majority. Locked into positions where their voices are not heard because others fear their potential, their confidence. A county that has always bled red and flaunts its power of whiteness has little to no regard for the success of others, be it adults or children.

The majority, white people, often band together in their silence even when they know it's wrong. The proof is in the pudding, especially when considering the last presidential election. I think most can agree his presidency heightened racial tensions in America, but the majority continued to support his illogical recklessness.

For years now, Black women have been overlooked and pushed out due to the systemic racism that plagues our school district. The breeding grounds of the white rooms are silent killers to Black and brown people, especially women. Stress, panic attacks, low self-esteem, weight gain and anger; yes anger, are just a few major side effects. White women, like Karen and Becky are known to create hostile environments; while others choose to remain silent and pretend to be oblivious.

Surprisingly, the same man that gave me the opportunity to climb the ladder, was the puppeteer for them to knock me down, *again*. Damn, that hurt!

Today, there are NO Black female principals at any of our secondary schools, middle or high. These jobs are generally set aside for white women and men, both young and old. The average age for most is between 30 - 35 years old. Young whites are often molded to be the next best or great leaders within the school district, often given questions to perform well on interviews, sometimes given mock interviews to seal their positions. While most Blacks don't see a promotion until their late thirties, early forties.

Black men are sometimes given these secondary opportunities while Black women are often placed at the elementary level requiring more work and less pay. These promotions are to be viewed as successes; however, it seems to be an age-old (good ole boy) tactic to keep everyone quiet.

A few years ago two female Assistant Principals (AP's), one Black and one white were given promotions. To my understanding, they both began their AP careers in the secondary sector around the same time and shared ideas here and there.

However, when promoted to principal, one made it to the high school level and the other elementary level. I'll allow my readers to put that puzzle together. Most notably, people know that's a substantive pay gap. Hidden racism, not hardly. White district leaders are very strategic in giving us enough to keep us quiet. These are the blatant disrespectful racial chess moves that are played out on the education plantation.

Seemingly, [for us] an administrative position is unfathomable let alone attainable, because our white counterparts view us as unintelligent and incapable of successfully holding such positions. These positions are as white as the cotton fields Blacks were beaten to plow with their bare hands. How can we expect our children to want more when we are barely represented in such positions?

I salute all of the Black and brown women who continue to fight this struggle of oppression, equity, depression, humiliation, belittlement and many other microaggressions faced in the workplace. I am now at peace as I make my exit from these abusive environments. This silent killer plagued me while working in administration. My next steps aren't completely certain, but I know, "God has a Plan!" I have no more tears to give! I have been forced to walk away from a profession I once loved and a career that I worked my ass off to secure. I cannot and will not continue to let *them* take my voice or my power with their diabolical lynching.

Take the Noose Off Challenge: Most learn the vowels of the alphabet at a very young age; yet forget them as they matriculate through life. We must go back and reflect on Vow(els) of Education:

A - Acknowledge to accept.
E – Empathize and execute sustainable solutions.
I - Identify to implement small steps daily.
O - Offer solutions to solve problems.
U - Unlearn problematic behaviors.

About the Author

Rometha Gilmore is the one and only Mrs. Educator. As a Black woman in leadership, her journey in public education began in Marion County Public Schools. Rometha is a zealous motivational speaker, educational consultant, advocate, and mentor to adolescent girls and women.

Her professional tenure within public education has been well-developed over the past two decades. Mrs. Educator has stood on the frontlines of education as a classroom teacher, dean of students, then transitioning into the role of an assistant principal.

Currently, Rometha resides in Ocala, Fl. with her husband and best friend who is also her high-school sweetheart, Jamie Sr. Together they have three sons, Eddie, Jamie Jr., and Jyron, three grandchildren and one goddaughter. Her family is the center of her happiness and the reason she advocates for all students as well as herself and colleagues. She enjoys quiet time with God, serving alongside her husband in ministry, shopping, line dancing, vacationing, and hanging out with her family in the backyard.

Mrs. Educator's mantra is simple, if we do not address crumbling family structures, communities, and the educational system, the knots in the noose will only tighten— and she refuses to stand by and watch this happen!

Printed in the USA
CPSIA information can be obtained
at www.ICGtesting.com
LVHW070411090224
771314LV00021B/56